Moe's Oboe

The Sound of OE

By Kara L. Laughlin

2

Oh no!
Moe lost his oboe.

Where could it be?

4

5

Look!
In the grass.
Is that Moe's oboe?

No. It is a hoe.

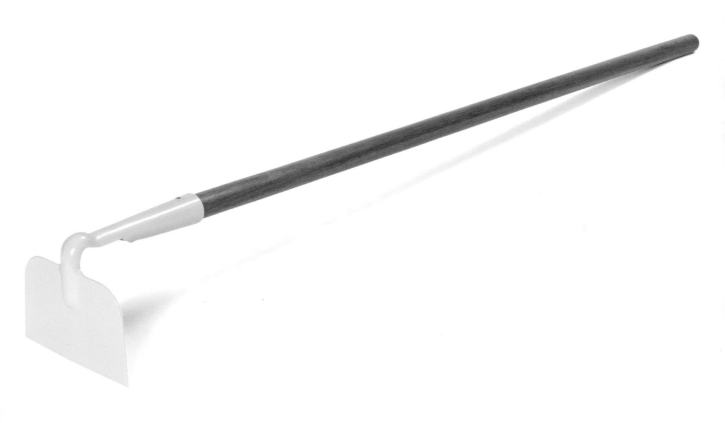

9

10

Listen!
By the pond.
Moe tiptoes over.

Is that Moe's oboe?

13

14

No. It is a doe.

Moe goes home.

17

Ow! Moe bumps
his toe.

19

Look!
On the floor.
It is Moe's oboe!

21

Word List:

doe	oboe
goes	tiptoes
hoe	toe
Moe	

Note to Caregivers and Educators

The books in this series are based on current research, which supports the idea that our brains are pattern-detectors rather than rules-appliers. This means children learn to read easier when they are taught the familiar spelling patterns found in English. As children encounter more complex words, they have greater success in figuring out these words by using the spelling patterns.

Throughout the series, the texts allow the reader to practice and apply knowledge of the sounds in natural language. The books introduce sounds using familiar onsets and *rimes*, or spelling patterns, for reinforcement.

For example, the word *cat* might be used to present the short "a" sound, with the letter *c* being the onset and "_at" being the rime. This approach provides practice and reinforcement of the short "a" sound, as there are many familiar words made with the "_at" rime.

The stories and accompanying photographs in this series are based on time-honored concepts in children's literature: well-written, engaging texts and colorful, high-quality photographs combine to produce books that children want to read again and again.

Dr. Peg Ballard
Minnesota State University, Mankato

Published by The Child's World®
1980 Lookout Drive • Mankato, MN 56003-1705
800-599-READ • www.childsworld.com

PHOTO CREDITS
© Andrew Burgess/Shutterstock.com: 9; Breadmaker/
Shutterstock.com: 17; Gelpi/Shutterstock.com: 2, 5, 10,
18; Kenneth Summers/Shutterstock.com: 6; Matthias
G. Ziegler/Shutterstock.com: cover, 21; Michal Kocan/
Shutterstock.com: 13, 14

ISBN 9781503835443
LCCN 2019944823

Printed in the United States of America

ABOUT THE AUTHOR

Kara L. Laughlin is an artist and writer
who lives in Virginia with her husband,
three kids, two guinea pigs, and a dog.
She is the author of two dozen nonfiction
books for kids.